ACKNOWLEDGEMENTS

The Host of Volunteers who made this book possible includes:

Ms. Jennie Walker Baird, Mrs. Frank Creekmore, Ms. Sandy Flatford, Ms. Alice L. King, Mr. Dennie Littlejohn, Mr. Curtis Lyons, Mr. Mac McDougald, Mr. Joe C. Rader, Mr. Eric Stinnett, Mr. W. Miles Wright.

Dr. Clint Allison, Mrs. Leonard Ambrose, Mr. John M. Armistead, Ms. Jeanne Barkley, Ms. Evelyn Blau, Ms. Anne Bridges, Mr. Emile Catignani, Dr. Jefferson Chapman, Ms. Mary Frances Crawford, Ms. Margaret Crawford, Ms. Claire Eldridge, Ms. Carol Evans, Mr. Bud Ford, Mrs. George T. Fritts, Sergeant Major Thomas Gage, Mr. Tom Garritano, Ms. Lori A. Goetsch, Ms. Rosita Gonzalez, Mr. David Harkness, Ms. Camille Hazeur, Mr. Robert Heller, Mrs. Cletus L. Jasper, Ms. Joan F. Jones, Ms. Claire Keene, Mr. Warren Kennerly, Mr. Jim Kelly, Dr. Tom Klindt, Dr. Suzanne Kurth, Ms. Angie W. LeClercq, Ms. Suzanne Livingood, Dr. Milton Klein, Ms. Lea Ann Law, Ms. Anne J. Lester, Mrs. Ralston Matheny, Dr. Anne Mayhew, Ms. Jeanne P. McDonald, Mrs. J. Stanley Miller, Mrs. Kyle C. Moore, Dr. Linda Painter, Ms. Sally Polhemus, Ms. Jane Pope, Mr. Neal O'Steen, Dr. Joan Paul, Dr. Jack Reese, Ms. Jackie Robinette, Mr. Ernest B. Robinson, Jr., Ms. Martha E. Rudolph, Dr. Mac Simpson, Mrs. Lynn Snyder, Ms. Betty Stuart, Colonel Thomas Trotta, Mr. and Mrs. Roberts Weaver, Ms. Susan W. Williams, Ms. Ethel Wittenberg, Dr. Dhyana Ziegler.

ISBN NUMBER :1-884850-00-6

Library of Congress Catalog Card Number: 94-65024
FIRST EDITION

BETSEY B. CREEKMORE

Betsey Creekmore, Associate Vice Chancellor for Business and Finance, is a native Knoxvillian. She is a graduate of Vassar College and Wesleyan University (Connecticut). The daughter of Knoxville historian Betsey B. Creekmore and the late Frank B. Creekmore, she is the great niece of former UT President James D. Hoskins. Her twin brother, David, is a Knoxville attorney.

SAM VENABLE

Sam Venable is a Knoxville native and a journalism graduate of The University of Tennessee. Both his mother, Mary S. Venable, and his father, the late Samuel A. Venable, were graduates of The University of Tennessee, where his father later taught physical education. Venable and his wife, Mary Ann, are parents of two children, Clay, 21, and Megan, 19, both students at The University of Tennessee. Venable writes a general interest column for The Knoxville News-Sentinel.

Cover Photographed by Michael Patrick

PHOTOGRAPHS BY

Paul Efird, Al Fuchs, J. Miles Cary, Julie Elman-Roche, Michael Patrick, Mike DuBose, Fritz Hoffmann, Bill Dye, Jack Kirkland, Dave Carter, and through the courtesy of UTK.

William Blount, Governor of the federal Territory South of the River Ohio from its inception in 1790 until Tennessee became a state in 1796. In 1794, America's first Territorial Legislature chartered "Blount College" which is now The University of Tennessee.

200 TENNESSEE
A CELEBRATION OF 200 YEARS OF THE UNIVERSITY

Text By
BETSEY B. CREEKMORE

Introduction By
SAM VENABLE

Edited & Designed by
J. BRUCE BAUMANN

INTRODUCTION

By SAM VENABLE

IF members of The University of Tennessee's class of 1900 could visit the Knoxville campus on a typical football Saturday, they'd surely be shocked speechless by the changes.

The sheer number of students, for one thing. UTK's current enrollment would have made up a whopping 77 percent of the entire city's population at the turn of the century. Throw in a 1994 campus stretching from the Tennessee River eastward to downtown, multiplied millions of dollars worth of buildings and facilities, the mania of Volunteer football, not to mention automobiles, computers, VCRs, ATMs and ... well, you get the picture.

But you know what just might surprise the returning grads more than anything else? The tidal wave of orange that floods the campus each fall.

You see, even though the university's official colors had been picked for a field day in 1889 ... in honor of orange and white daisies growing in profusion on The Hill ... members of the class of '00 had their own ideas. They chose purple and white as their standard. The class of '02 followed up with pink and lavender. Pink? I think not. Indeed, I shudder at the very thought.

This delightful nugget of UT trivia is one of dozens Betsey Creekmore unearthed while researching the text for this book. Did you know campus rules in 1821 expressly prohibited such heinous acts as dueling and wearing women's clothes? Or that "Uncle Jake," a Confederate veteran, once sold fruits and veggies from a pushcart and regaled students with war stories? Or that the UT Board of Trustees refused to install a telephone because it was "unneeded"? Or that hens from the school's poultry department held two egg-laying records? Or that chemistry professors discovered a Science Hall classroom that had been permanently sealed, apparently the academic version of retiring an athletic number?

If not, then it is my privilege to invite you for a stroll through two centuries at UT and my honor to introduce you to your guide.

Betsey Creekmore's name is virtually synonymous with The

4

University of Tennessee. Currently the associate vice chancellor for business and finance, her affiliation with the university stretches back to the mid-'60s, when she was a proofreader for the UT Press. A native Knoxvillian, she is a bubbling fountain of knowledge about the institution and its people and was a natural selection to compile the text when Scripps Howard Publishing and UT agreed to publish a book to celebrate the university's bicentennial. "Celebrate" is a key word here, for this is a joyous walk of the life and times of The University of Tennessee. This is not, however, your standard history book. The 129 pictures on these pages are not what you'd find in a typical historical review. All the facts and photographs are accurate, of course, but rather than providing a dry, chronological look at the evolution of UT, Creekmore and editor J. Bruce Baumann have served up a hearty stew from an incredibly wide variety of ingredients.

Through carefully selected vignettes, this book looks at UT during war and peace; the serious pursuit of education and silly college capers; the struggling days of Blount College and the birth of the statewide university system.

You will revisit the nostalgic years of Ellis and Ernest drugstore; the warm, wonderful presidency of Andy Holt; the strife that rocked UT, Knoxville and the nation during the turbulent 1960s; Vince Staten's abortive quest for Homecoming queen; the dreaded Junior English Exam; plus panty raids, the Ag Barnwarmin', bowl games, the Home Ec "practice house" and hundreds of other elements that have been so much a part of Big Orange Country for 200 years.

Ah, yes ... orange.

Just for the sake of argument, let me point out that during the pink and lavender era, a Volunteer player named A.H. Douglas punted a football a full 100 yards. Now, doesn't that make you want to leap to your feet, wave your shaker and scream, "Go Big Pink!" at the top of your lungs?

Me neither.

Sam Venable is a columnist for The Knoxville News-Sentinel, UTK '69.

1794. In China, it's the year of the tiger. George Washington is serving his second term as president of the United States of America. Congress authorizes formation of the U.S. Navy. Golf, croquet, tennis and cricket are popular in New York. Harvard admits its 158th class. Eli Whitney patents the cotton gin; Robert Fulton invents a marble-cutting machine. Born are William Cullen Bryant, Cornelius Vanderbilt and, to Gov. and Mrs. William Blount of the federal "Territory South of the River Ohio," a daughter, Eliza Indiana.

On the frontier, where the Cherokees of the Lower Towns had declared war on the United States two years earlier, The Knoxville Gazette, like the territorial capital city it serves, is 3 years old. It carries the news of the birth of the Blounts' daughter and reports the events of the Territorial Assembly, called with a view to petitioning for statehood. On Sept. 10, 1794, the Gazette announces the assembly has chartered a college in Knoxville with the unusual provision that students of all religious denominations may attend. Named Blount College to honor the governor near whose home the assembly convened, the institution that would become The University of Tennessee is launched.

From a handful of students enrolled in the Knoxville seminary of the Rev. Samuel Carrick — whose orations and declamations were interrupted by bursts of martial music and the practice firing of cannons from the Knoxville Blockhouse fort — the story of UT is one of students, faculty, staff, alumni and friends.

The institution's early history as Blount College and, in 1807, East Tennessee College, reveals efforts to survive, plus initial linking of the institution to the state and a classical curriculum similar to those of Harvard and Yale. It included the raising of money in a frontier town to build a two-story building on its main street; admission of the nation's first female students in 1804; and the 1810 attempt to enlist U.S. President James Madison and former President Thomas Jefferson as ticket sellers in a financially unsuccessful lottery to benefit the college. Other highlights from that period were the 1826 purchase of 40 acres of land and the relocation of the college to the site that a century later Mary Fleming Meek would characterize in the alma mater as "a hallowed hill in Tennessee."

Student conduct at East Tennessee College was governed by strict rules prohibiting blasphemy; robbery; fornication; theft; forgery; dueling;

The circa 1795 Blount College building near the northwest corner of frontier Knoxville's Town Square [corner of Gay and Clinch Streets] constructed with funds raised by public subscription. In use by Blount College/East Tennessee College until the 1828 move to The Hill.

assaulting or wounding the president or tutor; maliciously breaking the windows or doors of the faculty; wearing women's clothing; fraud; and lying. Students complained about the college's move because of the long walk or horseback ride from downtown boarding houses and the climb up what has come to be known as The Hill.

President Joseph (called "Old Joe" out of earshot) Estabrook, who was "given to elegant ruffles and fine boots, to the prodigious use of snuff, and to shooting even on Fast-Day," reshaped the curriculum, built on-campus dormitories and loaned the city of Knoxville $30,000 from college coffers to build a waterworks.

1864 view from inside the breastworks of Fort Sanders, showing the buildings of the closed East Tennessee University. The original locust, cedar, mulberry, and poplar trees were used for firewood as Confederate and Union troops successively occupied the campus.

East Tennessee College became East Tennessee University in 1840, a change President Estabrook sought as a way to distinguish the institution from academies or common schools and to allow establishment of a medical department, a move that did not come about for four decades. During the 10 years he served as president, running water came to the top of The Hill, pumped in an erratic stream through a 1/2 inch lead pipe to a single hydrant behind Old College; student literary societies flourished, published a magazine and invited young ladies from town (coeducation having lasted fewer than five years) to attend selected activities; a certificate program was begun to prepare teachers for the common schools and academies, admitting young men who were at least 16 years old and could read and write; and

a brief period of military discipline led to adoption of a student uniform and serious consideration of a faculty uniform.

W.D. Carnes accepted the presidency of East Tennessee University in 1858 on trustees' assurances that a gymnasium would be built and local citizens would see that no alcoholic beverages were sold to students. The gym, one of the nation's first, was built.

The university was in session when the Civil War began in April 1861. Overall, East Tennessee sympathized with the Union. Loyalties were divided, often within families, and students answering the calls for volunteers found themselves at war with their classmates. The university opened for the fall term, but without running water, "in consequence of the removal of the lead pipe by Confederate authorities." In January 1862, university facilities were commandeered by the Confederate Army for housing and hospitals. East Tennessee University closed for the duration of the war.

When the Union Army took Knoxville in September 1863, the university's trustees tried unsuccessfully to collect rent and damages from the Confederate government — even as the Union Army was using the campus as bivouac area, hospital and battlefield. When the fighting ended in 1865, the campus was a shambles. The locust, cedar, mulberry and Lombardy poplars had been cut down for firewood. Trenches laced The Hill on all sides. President Carnes' gymnasium had been razed by Union troops, and other university buildings were badly damaged. Records, equipment and library materials had been pilfered.

Nearly bankrupt, the trustees now sought compensation from the United States government for damages to buildings and grounds. The university operated for a year in the former "Deaf and Dumb Asylum" (later the Knoxville City Hall) while minimal repairs were made to campus buildings. The fall term of 1866 opened on a still-scarred campus. There were 88 students, all in the preparatory department. Two years later, student labor (at a wage of 10 cents an hour) helped to sod and grade the grounds and to plant 329 trees to begin to erase the war's effects. Seven years later, Congress appropriated $18,500, not as payment for damages, but in "full compensation for aid given by and on behalf of the University to the Army of the United States in the late rebellion."

An 1867 special act of Congress allowed Tennessee to participate in the program of land grants for agricultural education established by the Morrill Act of 1862, even though Tennessee had been part of the Confederacy at that time. In 1869, the Legislature designated East Tennessee University as the state's land grant institution, obligating the institution to acquire and operate a farm, emphasize education in agriculture and the mechanical arts, establish military training and offer the privileges of the university to qualified citizens of the state, regardless of race or color. The designation brought a welcome financial boost and changed the character of the institution's curriculum and culture.

East Tennessee University took seriously its obligation to provide military training. After the War Department's 1872 assignment of an instructor in military tactics, the campus operated as a military academy. Cadets wore uniforms similar to those of the U.S. Military Academy at West Point. They were required to participate in daily drills and inspections and operated under a system of military discipline. Restricted to campus unless they had a pass to leave, cadets found time in the highly regimented existence for midnight shootings of the two cannons that the War Department provided — shootings so frequent, in fact, the cannons were eventually moved to the farm.

Fraternities came to campus in 1872, with a one-year appearance of Alpha Tau Omega, and definitively when Pi Kappa Alpha organized in 1874. Intercollegiate athletic teams appeared in 1875 (the same year university buildings were lighted with gas) when the baseball club was organized. The team had its first undefeated season and beat one opponent by a score

The Hill, circa 1868, showing the results of student labor in grading the land and planting 166 forest trees (chestnuts and elms) and 163 evergreens.

of 63-17. The 1875 offering of the Cadet Dramatic Association included the skit "Fresh Fish's Troubles," a comic portrayal of a tongue-tied freshman. A cadet band was organized. Dancing became popular, giving rise to "military hops" and "farewell hops." Commencement was very elaborate (and hours long), beginning with a march of the cadets and faculty to the courthouse, where the trustees, mayor, aldermen, court and bar of the city and other leading citizens joined the parade to the Methodist Church.

East Tennessee University had been linked with the State of Tennessee since receipt of revenues from land sales as part of its transformation from Blount College to East Tennessee College. It had become Tennessee's land grant institution. It had received, however, not one dollar in state support. President Thomas Humes, the trustees and university supporters believed designation as Tennessee's state university would add prestige and might just lead the Legislature to appropriate funds. In 1879, the Legislature changed the name of the institution to The University of Tennessee, but the century would turn without an appropriation. That same year also marked the long-awaited establishment of a medical department, in Nashville, through designation of the former Medical College of Nashville as the "Medical Department of The University of Tennessee." A dental department, Tennessee's first and the nation's third, also was established in 1879.

Its first two decades as The University of Tennessee were years of considerable change. In 1881, 10 black students were appointed to legislative scholarships. Tennessee's 1870 Constitution prohibited integrated schools, but the land grant status mandated students be served regardless of race or color. For three years, trustees contracted with Fisk University to admit legislatively appointed students, with their Fisk tuition paid by UT. In 1884, UT established "The Industrial Department of The University of Tennessee" at Knoxville College, which operated until the "Tennessee Agricultural and Industrial Normal School for Negroes" (now Tennessee State University) opened in 1912.

The trustees, after initially turning down an "unneeded" telephone in 1881, installed one two years later on the faculty's recommendation. Dr. Charles Dabney, who had a "typewriting machine," became president, just in time to respond to a student rebellion and strike over the manual labor requirement of the practical agriculture course required for all students. Dabney agreed with the striking students (including future UT President James D. Hoskins) that the course content should be academic, and the program was changed to a standard classroom format.

Military discipline was dropped, and compulsory military instruction was required only for freshmen and sophomores. But Lt. Lawrence Tyson's "sham battles" were noisy and hotly contested events as cadets used blank artillery and rifle fire to hold or conquer The Hill. A new steam-heated science building was constructed, containing a 700-seat auditorium with a pipe organ. The Agricultural Experiment Station was established, and working on the university's farm became a popular means of student self-help. There was the new law department, with Professor Charles W. Turner, who delivered his law lectures around a large wad of chewing tobacco. The gymnasium lost during the Civil War was replaced by one in the new YMCA building, which also contained an indoor track and a bowling alley.

"Big Orange Country" had its beginnings in this period. In 1889, the school colors selected for the first field

In 1876, relatives and friends of cadets drove out from Knoxville to attend weekly dress parades. The parade ground and the Mess Hall were located on the site of the present-day Walters Life Sciences Building.

day were orange and white, same as the daisies that grew in profusion on The Hill. The first intercollegiate football game, a resounding defeat at the hands of Sewanee, was played in 1891. But the 1896 team proudly declared itself "Champions of Tennessee" following an undefeated season of four games, including a victory over the Chattanooga Athletic Association. The first UT annual was published on time in June 1897, although it had to be hastily reconstructed after copy and printing plates were destroyed in the April fire that gutted S.B. Newman Printing and other buildings in downtown Knoxville.

Coeducation returned, first in 1885 with the discovery that a cadet appointed to a legislative scholarship in the UT Industrial Department at Knoxville College was a woman. The university paid her tuition but relieved her of her "cadetship" and the military drill requirement. Faculty had indicated general support for admission of women as early as 1880. President Dabney favored the move. Mrs. Charles Perkins argued persuasively on philosophical grounds, and the potential for increased tuition revenues provided a strong pragmatic reason for change. In 1893, upon the faculty's formal recommendation (passed without a dissenting vote), the trustees adopted a policy of coeducation. Women quickly became academic leaders. In 1894-95, they won all the scholarship awards except the Allen Medal in mathematics.

The Hill in 1879, when *East Tennessee University* became *The University of Tennessee*.

As the century turned, the Farmer's Club required that candidates for membership must have "handled a hoe, rock'd a cradle, pulled a bell cord, and raised cane!" The Seventh Day Gourmand Club unabashedly publicized its purpose as being "the promotion of rotundity." The Budweiser Club and the University Bicycle Club (dedicated to "the building up of tissue") had both faculty and student members. The class colors of '00 were purple and white while the class of '02 chose pink and lavender.

The year of 1900 marked the establishment of Chi Omega sorority and the publication of professor Charles Ferris' "Manual for Engineers," which, by 1912, would be in its 18th printing. When funds were needed for engineering projects, Ferris was said to "rub his little book" to get advertisers for the next edition to provide either equipment or cash in return for the privilege of future inclusion.

There were still reminders of the Civil War. A Confederate veteran, known to the campus community as "Uncle Jake," rolled a pushcart to the top of The Hill each morning at 8 to sell fruits and vegetables and to tell stories about the bravery of both Union and Confederate soldiers. For years, students paid for Uncle Jake to attend the annual reunions of Confederate soldiers. Excavation began for the women's dormitory, Barbara Blount Hall. But work was halted when the burial ground for eight Union soldiers, identified by buttons and scraps of material, was discovered on the south slope of The Hill. Construction

Above: A typical cadet dormitory room of the 1890's. *Below:* 1892 football squad. (L-R) *Front Row:* Smith, Wegener, Fisher, Reed, Brown. *Second Row:* McSpadden, Ijams, Cox, Coach Cannon, Bates, Marfield. *Third Row:* Manager Dodge, Bell, White, L. Gebhardt, Rhea, Sims. *Top Row:* Duff, Ferris, Brown.

resumed only after the skeletons had been moved to the National Cemetery to marked but unidentified graves.

In 1901, Yale University awarded President Dabney the honorary doctor of law degree as part of its bicentennial observance. Meanwhile at UT, Dean Hoskins banned "bunny hugging," "turkey trotting" and "Boston dipping" following a freshman dance. The following year, A.H. Douglas punted a football 100 yards (on the 110-yard football field) in the Clemson game, and the nickname "Volunteers" — coined from Tennesseans' willingness to fight for their country in a number of earlier wars — was attached to UT athletic teams by an Atlanta newspaper.

This was also when the "Summer School of the South" held its first session. An initial attendance of 150 to 300 was expected. The campus was overwhelmed, however, when 2,019 teachers paid a registration fee of $5 to attend the six-week session. Lecture classes, held in a hastily erected outside pavilion, contained 500 to 1,000 students. The summer school program thrived for more than a decade as faculty including John Dewey, William Jennings Bryan and Jane Addams came to be part of the experiment.

The state made its first appropriation to the school in 1903 — $10,000 to purchase 36 acres of river-bottom land adjacent to the UT farm. The same year, Dabney accepted the presidency of the University of Cincinnati. Dabney recommended as his UT successor Dr. Brown Ayres, a member of the first Summer School of the South faculty, who had subsequently been offered a faculty position. Then serving as acting president of Tulane (and having declined the presidency of the University of Alabama), the native Tennessean

Angie Warren (Mrs. Charles) Perkins, first Dean of the Women's Department (1898-1900) served without compensation.

accepted the UT post in 1904.

During President Ayres' tenure, the Carnegie Library was built (its olive green walls and olive green linoleum "suggested the quiet and cleanliness of study"); student pressure resulted in installation of a public drinking fountain in Estabrook Hall; Tennessee Hall was acquired and renovated for the home economics department; students placed a horse skeleton attached to a wagon on top of Jefferson Hall as a Halloween prank; entrance requirements were raised; "colleges" and "departments" were established; library holdings approached 45,000 volumes; women were required to take physical education; the medical, dental and pharmacy units were moved to Memphis; and Harcourt Morgan and C.E. Brehm were among those who joined the faculty.

The Legislature began regular appropri-

UT President Brown Ayres with Mrs. Ayres and their eight children, 1915.

ations, culminating in the institution's first $1 million grant in 1917, just before war was declared. Male students volunteered, were drafted or returned to their homes to help with the wartime food drive. University women helped the Red Cross develop first aid training and other emergency services. Military training schools operated on campus. At the 1917 June commencement, President Ayres asked student James P. Hess to stand beside him and receive the diplomas of those not present. Hess held a double armload of diplomas when all names had been called.

Dr. Ayres died in 1919 before construction began on the building which bears his name; its dedicatory plaque twice misspells his name as "Ayers." Harcourt Morgan, dean of agriculture, was sworn in as president the same year, with James D. Hoskins to assist him as "dean of the university."

After World War I, the university welcomed veterans returning to pursue or continue education and instituted a program (including poultry raising) for disabled vets. Poultry quickly became a research area, and in 1927, two UT hens held world records: UT Queen, for consecutive laying for heavy breeds (111 days) and Lady Volunteer, for laying 279 eggs before going into molt.

In 1923, controversy arose. Two faculty dismissals touched off a dispute that led to the non-reappointment of five additional faculty, establishment of an underground student newspaper, petitions and letters directed to trustees and the Legislature, and harsh criticism from the Knoxville News.

The events were still being debated when, in 1925, the Legislature passed a bill prohibiting the teaching of evolution theory. Morgan, himself an evolutionist, declined to oppose the bill, a stand that writer Joseph Wood Krutch attributed to Morgan's concern "above all else with his precious appropriations." UT students responded to the bill with a satiric petition to the Legislature, suggesting that "the law of gravity be amended; that it be illegal to bring Fords into Tennessee; that Pi be changed to an even three; and that, since the Book of Revelation refers to the four corners of the earth, it should be illegal to teach that the world is round."

The campus was a lively place. In a two-day work project in 1921, students, faculty and administrators leveled, graded and installed a drainage system on Shields-Watkins Field. ALCOA loaned 200 picks, 200 shovels and 50 wheelbarrows for the effort. Dean Hoskins, L.R. Hesler, Charles Ferris and Nathan Dougherty were among the participants; Dr. William Holt of the hygiene department treated blisters.

Zollie Howard edited the 1924 Mugwump (the humor magazine so named by Howard H. Baker Sr.). Estes Kefauver was president of the All Students Club. In 1925, Pan Hellenic created the Nahheeyayli ("dance of the season") Club with required annual dues. "Buttonhole Nellie" Crooks presided at the Home Economics Building dedication and over the newly established "practice house." Students enjoyed the 1926 Ag Barnwarmin' at which hard cider was served and, contrary to widespread rumor, 'possum was not. This was the year UT changed from semesters to quarters and Capt. Robert R. Neyland was appointed football coach.

Bill Harkness won all the athletic prizes in 1927, and Everett Derryberry was named a Rhodes scholar. Dean F.M. Massey announced the number of allowable class cuts in any quarter "is limited to the number of times the class meets per week." In 1929, the annual carnival and circus were combined into a single event, "Carnicus," of which Pauline Buster was crowned queen. Eugene (Flash) McEver (of the Hack, Mac and Dodd backfield) was named UT's first All-American football player.

The stock market crash of 1929 was followed by the 1930 failure of Knoxville's Holston Union Bank, where some $400,000 of university capital and operating funds were on deposit. A few hours later, Nashville's Caldwell and Co. failed, with $7 million in state funds. The university shuffled money, borrowed money, cut expenditures and reduced salaries across the board. Room and board rates were lowered, and many students paid their tuition in installments.

During this same period, the yo-yo fad continued; the Orange and White added a rotogravure section; male freshmen wore traditional green caps with white "UT" and orange class numerals; and Dean Greve complained of the increase in cars on campus. But times were hard. Nahheeyaylis were canceled in 1933, and the Mugwump named "Miss Depression" as the most popular girl on campus. As many as 100 students would walk daily to the downtown Market House to purchase two corn muffins and a pint of milk for 10 cents. Students took any work offered, and selling a pint of blood brought $2.50. Class attire consisted of clothes on hand — for women, occasionally spike heels or party clothes.

In 1933, Harcourt Morgan was named to the board of the new Tennessee Valley Authority, and James D. Hoskins was appointed to succeed him as UT president. Managing the university was a budget-balancing act. Faculty, janitors and library assistants were let go. Senior faculty who resigned were replaced with junior faculty at lower salaries. Broken equipment could not be repaired. Faculty, teaching five or six courses per quarter on reduced salaries, frequently bought class materials for students.

In 1934, Coach Neyland was recalled to active duty. Two major fires occurred. The Morrill Hall fire destroyed the botany department's herbarium, a national treasure of more than 50,000 plant specimens. When Jefferson Hall, a wooden building rented to the Tennessee National Guard as an armory, caught fire, the ammunition stored there exploded, resulting in a spectacular (and frightening) fire. In 1935, Leonard Rogers was the first president of the All Students Club to be married while in office; football captain DeWitt Weaver was also married. In 1936, Maj. Neyland returned for his second term as football coach/ROTC instructor.

Impending flooding of former Indian burial grounds and town sites led to a TVA-UT-Tennessee Emergency Relief Administration partnership to create a program of anthropology to preserve and document sites that would be inundated. T.M.N. Lewis and Madeline Kneberg began work.

In 1938, at the urging of Dr. Ruth Stephens and upon the reluctant recommendation of Dean Greve, two women were named to the cheerleading squad (and were allowed to wear culottes for cheering). The nation sang about "three little fishes in an iddy biddy pool" but attributed the ditty to Saxie Dowell, not to its rightful UT authors Jo Carringer, Teddy Boman and Berenice Iddens. At the 1939 Aloha Oe, Tom C. Smith was named Volunteer of the Year. More than 10,000 people were in the stands as the 500 seniors processed from Shields-Watkins Field with their flickering candles to form a "T" on The Hill. As taps was played, the crowd silently dispersed and the difficult 1930s came to a close.

New Year's Day 1940 found a large contingent of UT football fans in Pasadena, Calif., for the Vols' first Rose Bowl appearance. Among them were two members of the band who had hitchhiked from Knoxville in their bright orange uniforms. Back in Knoxville, students were concerned about the country's closeness to war, but a major January snow offered an opportunity to pepper faculty with snowballs and form the "to-class-by-sled club." An electric grading machine installed in the registrar's office provided automated scoring of test answers placed on "nonconductive" paper with "electrographic lead" pencils. The chemistry faculty discovered and reopened a Science Hall room that had been permanently sealed, following the death of Professor Wait, apparently an academic version of retiring the numerals of outstanding athletes. The Junior English Exam was given, and singer Bing Crosby selected the year's "Volunteer Beauties."

Fall brought dedication of the Ayres Hall floodlights and chimes, a change from compulsory chapel to "voluntary assembly" and a day's suspension of classes to allow male students to register as required by the Selective Service Act. Robert Earl Ogle, the UT farm foreman's son, reported for duty on four hours' notice; he was the first student to be drafted. President Hoskins announced full tuition refunds for those conscripted or called to duty. In December, the football team received a bid to the Sugar Bowl.

When war was declared in 1941, Vic Davis, executive director of the Alumni Association (annual dues: $2), notified members that efforts would focus upon communications with UT servicemen. Hand-addressed monthly to a list that grew to more than 7,000, "The Hill-O-Gram" sent news from UT (including the popular football "Dyergrams" by Knoxville News-Sentinel cartoonist Bill Dyer before he left for duty), plus lists of military promotions or assignments of alumni. On campus, war bond stamp days were Tuesdays. The basketball team won the first of two consecutive SEC titles. Blackouts were enforced, and the UT library turned out its lights from 8:30 to 9:30 each evening to save electricity. Dean Greve announced "there is no rule or regulation which obliges sparking couples to separate for the duration of the blackout."

Enrollment declined. By 1943, when UT's state appropriation rose to the 1929 level, women outnumbered men 2 to 1. An estimated 6,500 former students and 22 faculty were on active duty. Actual enrollment was a military secret because some students were on campus through military training programs. The university again took on the appearance of a military institution as bugle calls rang out, soldiers drilled and Alumni Gym and East Stadium were converted into barracks.

The extension division offered courses to employees of the mysterious installation at Oak Ridge, whose secretly large work force caused unusual area shortages. The College of Agriculture stressed Victory Gardens. Crepe paper decorations, homecoming floats and Nahheeyaylis "went to war" with gasoline and nylon stockings. One student came to campus on horseback, tethering her mount behind Ayres Hall.

In 1944, UT celebrated both its sesquicentennial (theme: "The University of Tennessee — Yesterday, Today, and Tomorrow") and the return of football after cancellation of the 1943 season for lack of players. The 1944 team earned Tennessee's second bid to the Rose Bowl, a second loss to Southern Cal. In 1945, UT and the nation celebrated the end of World War II, taking pride that the "secret city" of Oak Ridge and scientists such as UT's William Pollard had helped bring it to a close.

A flood of returning veterans arrived on a campus which had seen no major new buildings since the early 1930s and had lost four structures to fire in the meantime. There was not enough dormitory housing and no housing at all for married students. There was one campus cafeteria and no student center. Campus landscaping was unceremoniously disturbed by student housing: 175 trailers on The Hill and an additional 125 along Kingston Pike. Prefabricated Army barracks became houses, classrooms, offices and a student center.

In July 1946, following a successful public battle with Gov. Jim McCord about increasing the UT appropriation, 76-year-old President Hoskins retired. He was succeeded by Agriculture Dean Cloide Everett Brehm, whose first fall quarter as president would see physical and human resources of the institution swamped by an enrollment of 7,300 (3,500 freshmen; 4,901 veterans). For the first time in UT history, qualified students were denied admission when Brehm announced no new freshmen or sophomores would be admitted for winter quarter. New regulations banned freshmen parking on campus and established student parking areas (expressly excluding the top of The Hill). The penalty for a violation was a ticket and loss of parking privileges for the duration of enrollment.

As Howard H. Baker Jr. assumed the presidency of the student body in 1948, the university was bracing for a decade of construction. By 1959, UT would complete eight new, large academic buildings on the main and agricultural campuses; make major additions to four buildings; add one dormitory with another under way; buy an apartment complex on Chapman Highway for married students; and add a student center, a field house/armory, a theater-in-the-round and a Hearing and Speech Center. Mud, noise and heavy construction equipment were everywhere as barracks and trailers slowly gave way to permanent facilities.

Faculty such as Ruth Stephens, David VanVactor, Kermit Ewing, Alwin Thaler, John C. Hodges, "Jimmy" Walls, Philip Hamer, Jessie Harris, Theodore Glocker, Frank Ward, William E. Cole, Kenneth Hertel, Robert Boarts, Stanley Folmsbee, Neal Peacock, LeRoy Graf

and Kenneth Curry provided stability for the changing university, and athletic events added spirit. Gen. Neyland's teams were famous for the single wing and brutal defensive attacks. In 1951, nearly everyone in Tennessee knew the names of Hank Lauricella and Andy Kozar as the Vols reigned as national champions. Students wore "rooter caps" of orange and white to the games while the card section provided intricate displays.

Gen. Neyland left head coaching duties for the athletic director's position in 1952. The same year, Eugene Mitchell Gray, Knoxville College graduate, became the first black student to be enrolled on campus as the trustees complied with a court order to admit black students to the graduate school and College of Law. Lilly Jenkins was the first black person to receive a UT campus degree, the master's in special education, in 1954.

Students were required to check their "distribution boxes" daily and to respond within 48 hours to official notices placed in them. Unofficial news spread quickly as students used Ellis and Ernest, Byerley's and the T-Room for eating and gathering. In 1950, Chi Omega installed permanent Westminster Chimes in Ayres Tower, replacing those installed as part of the Massey Memorial Organ; Sigma Alpha Epsilon's 3-month-old lion mascot, loaned by the Knoxville Zoo, spent a day at large on the campus while fraternity members responded to reports of "sightings"; and Dr. Paul Soper announced the UT Theater would have a touring company, taking Thornton Wilder's "Our Town" to Harriman, Jellico, Oak Ridge and Athens.

By 1956, the decision had been made not to merge Memphis State into UT;

the new "isotopic" hospital, which could take advantage of research opportunities with Oak Ridge, stood as a memorial to Tennessee's World War II veterans; a rapidly spreading blight had killed a dozen of the more than 300 campus elms; and Marion Greenwood, nationally prominent artist, had completed a 5-by-28-foot mural in the ballroom of the University Center. On-campus parking was a major, and increasing, problem.

Seven students were expelled in spring quarter 1959 following a late-night panty raid that reached near-riot proportions. In the dim light, students came to blows over "trophies" that fluttered down from windows of the women's dorm. In better light, one of the hard-won trophies turned out to be a washcloth.

Following the spring quarter, President Brehm retired. His trademark bow tie was supplanted by the orange blazer of his successor, Dr. Andrew D. Holt. Audiences throughout the state and the nation laughed as Dr. Holt joked about "Martha's paper route," which his UT salary augmented; believed when he forcefully presented the needs of the university, citing well-chosen facts that substantiated his claims; and embraced The University of Tennessee as an extension of its charismatic president.

The Holt era was characterized by exploding growth — in facilities, funding, enrollment, faculty and staff — and by clashes related to national and local issues. Unlike the scene at many other college campuses in the 1960s, dissent did not escalate into riots although exuberance over athletic victories or snow occasionally did.

Picketing, rallies or demonstrations were held over a wide variety of issues — integration of area eating establishments; a greater voice for black students in university governance and activities; establishment of ROTC programs in local high schools; policies of the Selective Service related to the Vietnam War; UT's speaker policy (ruled unconstitutional by U.S. District Court in a lawsuit brought by students); design of the Volunteer statue, criticized by art students as "archaic" (resulting in design changes before casting); a new trademark on university signs, replacing the traditional interlocking "UT"; and curfews in women's residence halls (replaced by a system of differentiated housing).

In 1961, UT began the celebration of the Land Grant University Centennial. Integration of the undergraduate school went smoothly as three black students enrolled without incident. In 1962, UT supporters everywhere cheered Isabel Tipton's General Electric College Bowl team as it scored four nationally televised victories. John Cullum, Robert Preston and Jean Simmons came to campus to film "All the Way Home." The stadium was named for Gen. Neyland. Ray Mears became basketball coach.

Most members of the 1963 university community remember what they were doing when they learned on Nov. 22 that President John F. Kennedy had been assassinated. The campus mourned with the nation, suspended classes and held a requiem Mass in the University Center ballroom. Ann Baker (who in 1971 would become the first woman appointed to the UT Board of Trustees) was awarded a men's golf scholarship; a student activities fee, long sought and immediately unpopular, was instituted; and UT and the Knoxville Housing Authority agreed that the Yale Avenue Urban Renewal

Project would provide expansion land for the university.

In 1965, faculty and community members of Phi Beta Kappa finally obtained a chapter for UT; Social Security numbers were required for class registration; and the Orange and White became a daily newspaper (during the week), changing its name to The Daily Beacon. In a tragic consequence of a snowball fight, a UT student was shot and killed by a trucker who had been yanked from the cab of his vehicle. In 1967, compulsory ROTC was abolished, the Hunter Hills Theatre Repertory Company gave its first production and Ellis and Ernest drugstore was razed.

In 1968, Chris Whittle and Peter Kami ran on the same ticket for president and vice president of the student body. The ticket won the straw poll. In the real election, Whittle was elected president, but Kami was defeated by Ford Stuart for vice president. Also in 1968, Lester McClain became the first black UT football player.

At the same time, both the new campus and its future administrative structure began to take shape. The Martin campus, a UT branch since 1927; the new Chattanooga campus, formerly the University of Chattanooga; the medical units at Memphis; a new campus at Nashville, expanding the Knoxville extension program; and the Knoxville campus (with its affiliated Space Institute) became "primary campuses" headed by chancellors who reported to the president of the university system, as did vice presidents. Dr. Charles Weaver, dean of engineering, was named UTK chancellor.

In 1969, Jimmie Baxter became the first black student body president; UT celebrated its 175th birthday; and marijuana was discovered growing on the lawn of the University Center. Kappa Alpha fraternity closed the decade with a literal bang by firing a cannon blast that blew out almost all the windows of its house. And at the board of trustees' meeting in June, Andy Holt announced his retirement, effective Aug. 31, 1970.

The students of the late 1960s had achieved, by rallies and recourse to the courts, many changes on campus. They had made their views of national policy known in visible but peaceful ways. The first two years of the next decade were different.

In their search for a new president of the university system, the trustees had sought counsel from faculty and students. Ignoring the preferences of these people, however, trustees elected Dr. Edward J. Boling as president. Campus activist Peter Kami challenged the president-elect to a symbolic duel, and in January 1970, 2,500 students gathered on The Hill to protest Boling's selection. When demonstrators tried to enter the Administration Building, Chancellor Weaver ordered the crowd to disperse, finally calling for help from the police. A five-hour melee erupted; six people were injured and 22 arrested. Tear gas dispersed the crowd, first at the Administration Building, then at the Student Center where protesters had regrouped. Despite the rocky beginning of his administration, Dr. Boling served with distinction for 18 years.

In April, an anti-war rally at the downtown Post Office drew 400 picketers; 1,500 students protested the curfews in dormitories and regulations for off-campus housing; and rallies surrounding Earth Day were well-attended. A three-day strike was called by Jimmie Baxter to protest the Vietnam War, and classes were either canceled by professors or sparsely attended by students. In May, the Black Student Union presented demands for greater involvement in campus life at a rally of 300. The weekend of May 16 was one of serious vandalism as the Music Annex (a World War II barracks building on The Hill) was firebombed, a fire was set in South Stadium Hall and windows were broken in Stokely Athletic Center and the Humanities Building. The mural painted by Marion Greenwood, controversial among black students because it featured banjo-playing slaves in the West Tennessee segment, was damaged by paint and solvents.

While these events transpired, the campus had been preparing for a 10-day Billy Graham crusade to be held in Neyland Stadium. In 1969, 129,000 Knoxville-area residents had signed petitions inviting Graham in the culmination of a 17-year effort to bring a crusade to Knoxville. The dates were set for May 22-31. Thousands had been involved in preparations for the visit, and the Legislature had declared May 22, 1970, as "Billy Graham Day." Johnny Cash, Ethel Waters, Norma Zimmer and Bev Shea would be on the program. The UT band would play, and football coach Bill Battle would lead the pledge of allegiance to the flag.

At the invitation of Dr. Graham, President Richard Nixon announced he would be part of the May 28 service, his first public appearance on a college campus since the announcement that U.S. troops had entered Cambodia. The crusade filled the stadium every night. On the evening of May 28, 75,000 people were inside, 25,000 more outside, as Nixon and Graham walked onto the field. A group of approximately 200 protesters — mostly UT students and faculty with signs saying "Peace Now" and "Thou Shalt Not Kill" — booed and

jeered as the president spoke. Nine demonstrators were arrested for disturbing a public worship service. The protesters contended the appearance of Nixon constituted a political event, at which they were entitled to express their opinions.

The volatile year of 1970 also saw the abolition of the Junior English Exam; the replacement of Tartan Turf on the football field, which had turned from green to black; Ingrid Bergman on campus to film "A Walk in the Spring Rain"; the suspension of election of a Homecoming queen following the election (declared invalid) of Daily Beacon columnist Vince Staten; and appointment of the first black person to a central administrative post. In 1971, the opening performance of "Othello" was canceled minutes after it began as black students protested a white student playing the lead in blackface. Blind political science professor Otis Stephens shot a hole-in-one on par-three No. 6 at Colonial Golf Course. Chancellor Weaver resigned to become a vice president of the UT system.

Dr. Archie Dykes, UT-Martin chancellor who had been a strong candidate for president of the UT system, became the UTK chancellor. Dr. Dykes, an assiduous letter writer, followed even chance meetings with cordial notes and was a popular speaker throughout the state. During his two-year service as chancellor, campus housing regulations were modified; the first woman was appointed to a a central administration post; on-campus voter registration drives were held; the ombudsman's office was established; the first home football game at night was played before a record crowd of 71,647; David Edgar became UT's first Olympic Gold Medal winner as a member of the 400-meter freestyle swimming relay team; and the university purchased the house next door to the president's residence to be the chancellor's residence. A task force on women and a task force on blacks recommended improvements. Campus disturbances persisted, particularly related to the playing of "Dixie" at football games and to the display of the Confederate flag.

In 1973, Dr. Dykes accepted the presidency of the University of Kansas, and Dr. Jack Reese, associate vice chancellor for academic affairs, was named chancellor, a position he would hold for 17 years. During the 1970s, zoology professor David Etnier's discovery of the snail darter in the Little Tennessee River ultimately failed to stop completion of the Tellico Dam project; skateboards invaded the campus; and the personal computer rapidly changed ways in which records were kept, correspondence written, themes prepared and research projects completed.

Pat Head was appointed Lady Vols basketball coach in 1974, and women's athletics became a major part of campus life. Coach Ray Mears' basketball stars Ernie Grunfeld and Bernard King became a national sensation as the "Ernie and Bernie show," and coach Stan Huntsman ran the string of SEC track and field championships to 15, highlighted by the 1974 NCAA championship. In 1977, Johnny Majors came home, replacing Bill Battle as football coach; the Minority Engineering Program achieved nationally regarded success; classes were canceled because of snow for the first time since the 1960s; 117 students were assigned to "overflow" housing in fall quarter; and lines for registration and drop-add were exceptionally long.

In January 1980, black students escalated their call for divestiture of stocks of companies doing business in South Africa as well as their demands for greater involvement in university governance. The office of the dean of student activities was firebombed; the director of the Black Cultural Center was reassigned to the personnel office; 17 students who refused to leave the center were arrested; and closure of the center touched off protests.

The 1982 World's Fair left UTK several legacies, including a greatly enhanced east entrance to the campus, the world's largest Rubik's Cube, a camel saddle, three windmills, an anaerobic digester and a eucalyptus tree. During the fair, UT beat Alabama 35-28, the first victory over the Crimson Tide since 1970.

In the '80s, UTK sought to balance its roles as a land grant institution and Tennessee's state university. The policy of admitting all Tennessee high school graduates was replaced by a moderately selective admissions policy and high school courses required for admission were specified. In 1988, the semester system was re-established.

Also during this period, campus automatic teller machines were installed. Law college teams won two National Moot Court competitions. The Lady Vols basketball team won three national championships. Sweet success came in the 1986 Sugar Bowl as MVP Daryl Dickey led the underdog Vols over Miami 35-7; the 1986 Orange and White spring game broke national attendance records by drawing 73,801; and the Homecoming queen election was revived. Zoology professor Roland Bagby illustrated lectures with songs summing up their content. The sports arena was completed, and the Hodges Library was "renovated and expanded" into its ziggurat shape. Ties to Oak

Ridge were strengthened through the Department of Energy's process of seeking a new manager for the National Laboratory and other installations and by creation of the "Science Alliance" between UT and ORNL as a "Center of Excellence" under Gov. Lamar Alexander's innovative program. The state's "Chairs of Excellence" program provided funds to attract nationally prominent teacher-scholars.

In June 1987, President Boling announced his retirement, and in January 1988, former Gov. Alexander was elected to succeed him. The following year, Dr. Reese announced his intention to return to teaching. He was succeeded, in 1989, by Dr. John Quinn, dean of the faculty at Brown University and a highly respected physicist. Alexander had reorganized the UTK administration, and declining state revenues brought severe appropriations cuts. There were reductions in maintenance service, two years of no salary increases and a pervasive need to "do more with less." Class sizes increased, and the number of classes offered decreased.

The football team started its 1988 season 0-6, leading to widespread fan complaints and billboards saying, "GO VOLS! BEAT ANYBODY!" Once the spell was broken, however, the team rebounded with back-to-back SEC championships and victories in the Cotton and Sugar bowls. The success of the football team and the Lady Vols basketball team, the continuing climb of external funding for research projects, the national prominence of the alternative fuels vehicles built by engineering students and other achievements were insufficient counterbalances to declines in state funds and increases in student fees.

President Alexander was appointed U.S. secretary of education in 1991. Shortly after, popular, longtime UT administrator Dr. Joseph E. Johnson was named to succeed him. Dr. Quinn stepped down to assume a Chair of Excellence in the physics department. Dr. William T. Snyder, formerly dean of engineering and the player of the "Mighty Wurlitzer" organ at the Tennessee Theatre, was named chancellor, and Phillip Fulmer succeeded Johnny Majors as football coach.

The university today is alive with fax machines, E-mail messages, rollerbladers and the sorts of healthy debate and discussion that characterize all good universities. Freshmen no longer wear caps with class numerals, but they can be identified by the headsets necessary to take the required audiotape tour of the Hodges Library.

And here we are in 1994. On a bright blue day in October, when Neyland Stadium becomes Tennessee's sixth largest city, 97,000 people of various sizes wedge themselves into their allotted 16 inches of seating. All shades of orange form a blend that moves in time with "Rocky Top" and roars in response to a UT touchdown. Alumni and friends in near and distant places gather to watch or listen to the game. But the game is more symbol than present contest. It is the echo of times and people remembered; a recognition of struggle and celebration of achievement; and reassurance that the torch has been passed and is being carried high. The band forms the "UT" and begins to play the alma mater. Those who have been touched by the first 200 years of Tennessee's state university and land grant institution salute the past, present and future.

"So here's to you, old Tennessee ..."

THE LAST 100 YEARS

Old College, *above,* completed in 1828, first building on The Hill, circa 1900.

Field Day, *left,* 1894 (L-R): W.H. Gebhardt; Professor McCall; Professor Cooper D. Schmitt; and (clearing the bar) J.J. Bernard.

In 1899, this weather kite was an important "scientific instrument" of the weather station.

To offer a course in Meteorology, President Dabney arranged for the Knoxville Weather Bureau to relocate to campus. Chief Meteorologist Weston M. Fulton (UT Master's in Engineering, 1901; internationally recognized inventor) and students in the Old College tower's weather station, circa 1900.

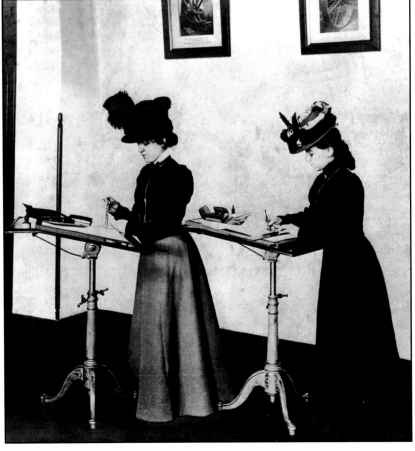

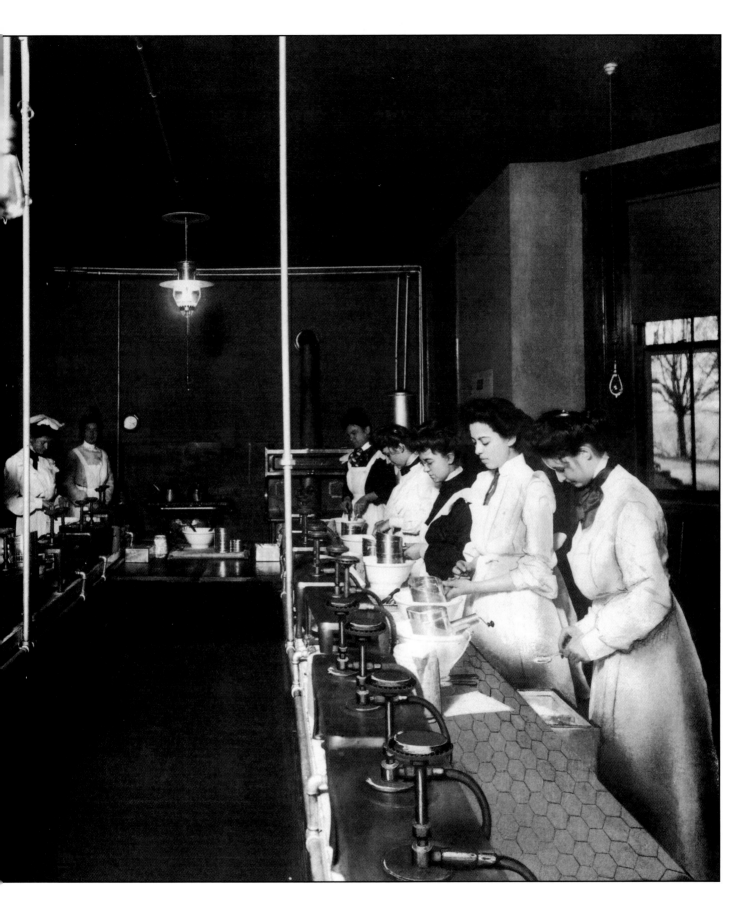

Circa 1905, women students at work in the related arts laboratory *(upper left)*; a mechanical drawing class *(lower left)*; and *(above)* in the domestic science laboratory in the basement of Barbara Blount Hall.

Maude Risenden, 1909, first woman to graduate from the College of Law, in academic regalia adopted for Commencements by the Law College in 1901 and by the rest of The University in 1903.

Dr. Charles Wait, professor of chemistry
and metallurgy, in his Science Hall
office with adjoining laboratory, 1914.

Barbara Blount Hall (pictured in 1915) was named for Governor Blount's daughter, one of the nation's first five coeds (Blount College, 1804). The other coeds were Polly McClung, Jennie Armstrong, Mattie Kain and Kitty Kain.

The entire University of Tennessee Marching Band, 1915.

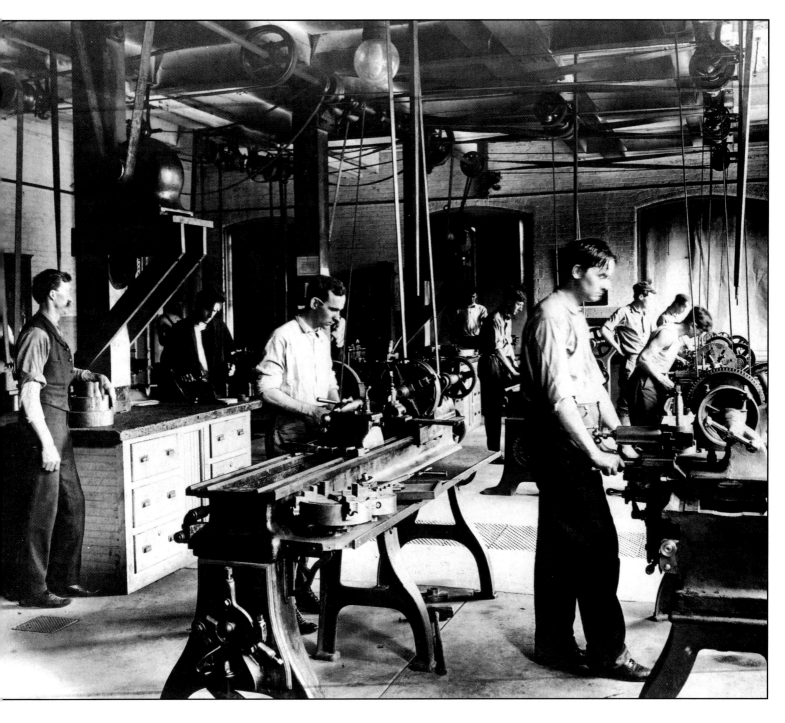

An Engineering Laboratory in
Estabrook Hall, circa 1920.

Dr. Brown Ayres, UT President
1904-1919, for whom The
University's landmark building
was named in 1921.

Estes Kefauver, Vol Tackle, 1922, the first year the football team wore orange jerseys. (Tackle 1922-23; Second Team All-Southern, 1923.) President of All Students Club. U.S. Senator from Tennessee and Adlai Stevenson's Vice Presidential running mate in 1952. Kefauver's papers are preserved in the Kefauver Special Collections Wing of UTK's Hoskins Library, along with a full-size recreation of his Senatorial Office.

Even after the 1921 "Class Days" project in which students, faculty, and administrators constructed Shields-Watkins field in two days, the drainage system worked erratically, and eventually had to be replaced.

From 1891 until the Alumni Memorial Gymnasium opened in the 1930's, the YMCA Building *(above)* housed The University's only indoor athletic facilities. These included a small swimming pool and *(left, circa 1915)* a two-story gym with an oval track at the balcony level.

Women on campus in the 1920's:
Above: 1922, compulsory chapel in
Science Hall auditorium. *Right, top:*
1923 Rifle Team. *Right, bottom:* The
1929 Golf Club.

UTK's proscenium theatre bears the name of Clarence Brown, 1910 UT graduate who directed some of the greatest motion pictures of all time. The estate plans of Clarence and Marian Brown provided UT's largest private gift to date, a $12,000,000 endowment for the UTK Theatre Department. Brown is pictured above with (L-R) Jean Harlow, Myrna Loy, and Clark Gable during the 1936 filming of *Wife versus Secretary*, and *at right* directing Greta Garbo.

BROWN·489
DANIELS

Gene McEver (the "Mac" of "Hack, Mac and Dodd"), wingback, 1928-29, 1931; All-Southern, 1928, 1930, 1931; All American, 1929; Hall of Fame. *Right:* 1935: The entire campus. On Saturday afternoons, trains crawled past on the nearby railroad tracks and passengers crowded the windows for a glimpse of the Tennessee Volunteers in action.

FOOTBALL, 1939: Above, top: UT 21, Alabama 0 — tailback Johnny Butler through the line of scrimmage on a 56 yard run. *Above, bottom:* Senior line (L-R) Coleman, Shires, Molinski, Ackerman, Suffridge, Luttrell, Cifers. *Right:* Dr. James D. Hoskins, UT President (1934-46) seated in Neyland Stadium's President's Box on the 50 yard line.

Skiing to class in the January 1940 snow.

1939 mid-winter Nahheeyayli
heart-and-arrow formation.

Becoming Tennessee's Land Grant institution required purchasing a farm and a focus upon agriculture. This circa 1946 aerial photograph shows the UT farm, now the Agriculture campus. At center left is the home of Dr. H.A. Morgan, who resigned as UT President in 1933 to become one of the first Directors of TVA.

Coeds pose on an antique car in 1947.

During World War II, when women outnumbered men 2 to 1, Sadie Hawkins' Day activities were particularly popular.

Following World War II, there was a housing crisis when thousands of veterans enrolled on the G.I. Bill. In 1946, trailer villages were hastily created on The Hill *(right)*, on Cumberland Avenue where the Law School is today, and at the Agriculture campus. *Above:* Mr. and Mrs. A.K. Williams were the first couple to move in. They were assigned Trailer #8 on Middle Drive.

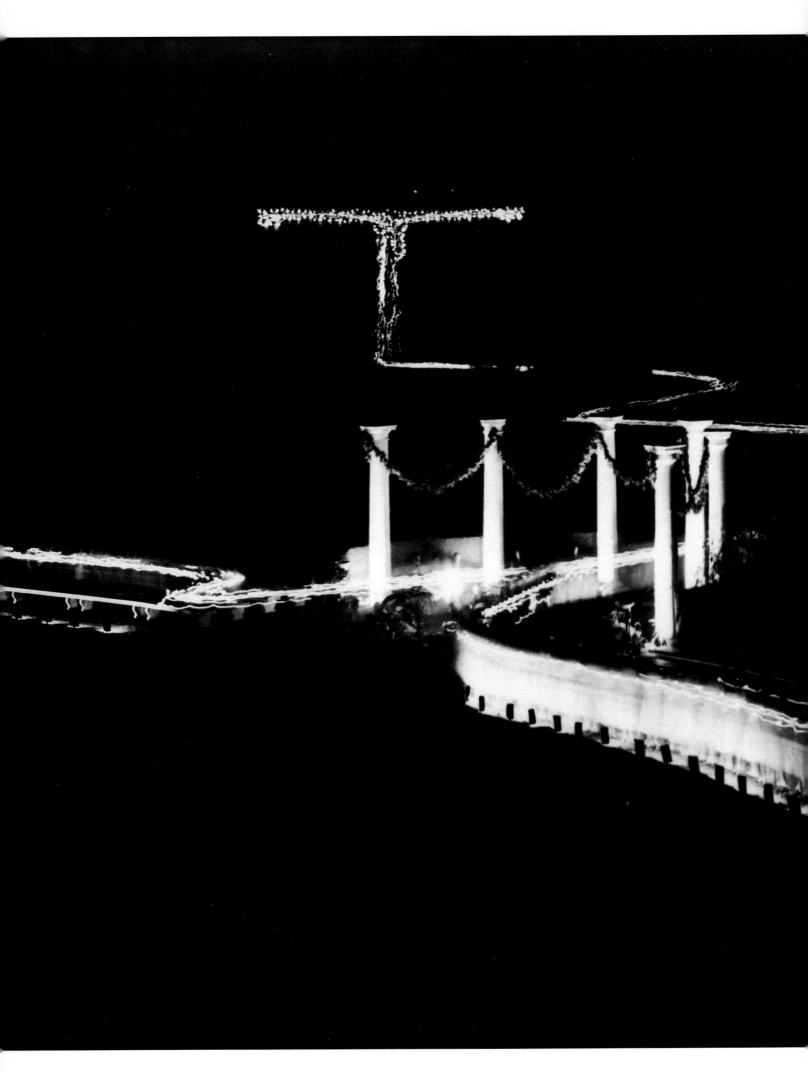

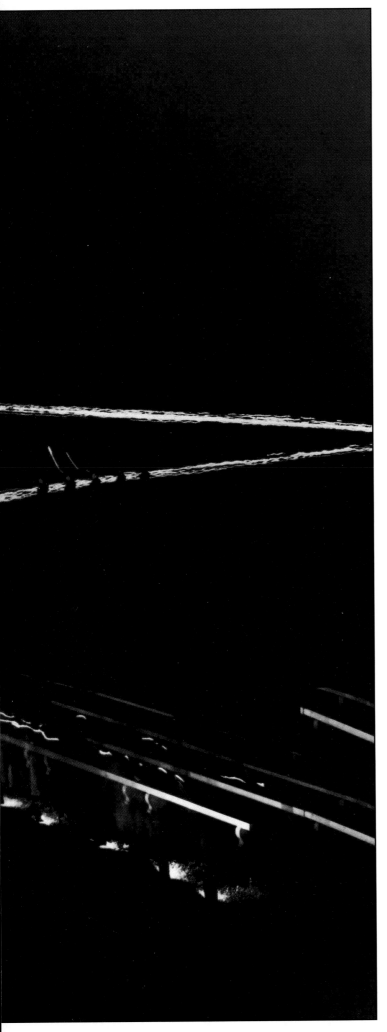

Players and Coach
Robert R. Neyland cele-
brate the 1949 6-0 win
over Kentucky. At the
1948 Aloha Oe, left,
Seniors form the candle-
light "T" on The Hill.

Top left: The Ellis and Ernest soda fountain, circa 1950. *Top right:* Tennessee's version of the *Stein Song*, 1953. *Above:* dorm room in Henson Hall, circa 1950. *Right:* 300-car student parking lot created on 15th Street, 1952.

Dr. Ruth Stephens, 1946. Professor of History and Political Science, Dr Stephens was a well known radio and television political analyst and a favorite civic group speaker.

Professor Forrest Lacey teaches a College of Law class, 1951.

In 1955, nationally prominent portrait artist Marion Greenwood, artist-in-residence 1954-55, puts finishing touches on a mural in the Carolyn P. Brown Memorial University Center which depicts the musical heritage of Tennessee. UT faculty, staff and students served as models. After the painting was vandalized in 1970, it was restored and covered with protective paneling.

In 1959, members of Phi Sigma Kappa fraternity sought to discover how many volunteers a telephone booth could hold.

Johnny Majors, (tailback, 1954-56; All Southeastern Conference, 1955,1956; All American, 1956; Southeastern Conference Player of the Year and runner-up for the Heisman Trophy) shown slipping by the defense in UT's 35-7 1956 defeat of Auburn. He returned to Neyland Stadium as head football coach in 1977 for a 16 year stay.

In its first tickertape parade since the end of World War II, Knoxville sent the 1962 GE College Bowl Team off for its fifth and final contest. Being showered by confetti are (L-R): Anne Dempster; Coach Isabel Tipton, Professor of Physics; and Joe Gorman. *Above:* The College Bowl Team (from left) Harold Wimberly, Joe Gorman, Anne Dempster, and David Rubin, with game show host Allen Ludden.

Fall, 1961: *Top Right:* Freshmen register for classes in Alumni Gym, unpursuaded by efforts by Phi Gamma Delta members *(above)* to divert them. *Right:* The homecoming parade along its downtown Knoxville route.

Delta Delta Delta sorority's 1961 Carnicus Skit, "Let's See 3-D." *Top right:* 1963 UT Singers. *Lower right:* Kathy Van Natlee and Gina Fornara, 1963, in the new Dunford Hall dormitory.

State-of-the-art technology in 1965: Dr.
Howard R. Pollio delivers a TV lecture to his
Psychology 212 class with the aid of Richard
Sentella, senior in Mechanical Engineering.

Also in 1965, Dr. William Bull teaches a General Chemistry class.

Above: Because the men's trophy was already on its way to the victory celebration, directors of the winning efforts in the 1967 All Sing large group division Helen Stewart (Alpha Chi Omega) and Chris Whittle (Phi Gamma Delta) shared a picture with the women's trophy.

Left: Dr. Nathan W. Dougherty, Dean of Engineering, is pictured in 1963 in front of the new Engineering Building named for him. Inset is a 1909 photograph of him as "Big Un" Dougherty, guard and sometimes fullback. As Chairman of the Athletic Council, he was responsible for finding and hiring Robert R. Neyland as football coach.

Above, right: Richmond Flowers, 1969, track and football standout. Track: SEC champion, indoor 60 yard high hurdles, 100 yard dash, and 120 yard high hurdles. NCAA championship, 1968, 60 yard high hurdles. Football: wingback, 1966-67; tailback, 1968; All-American, and All Southeastern Conference, 1967.

Above, left: Three freshmen 1969 UT majorettes (L-R): Karen Crumm, Debbie Holloway, and Susan Douglas.

Right: In 1968, the year Tennessee played the nation's first collegiate football game on artificial turf, wide receiver Lester McClain (1968-70) was UT's first black varsity football player.

The cake reads:

LEGEND
ACADEMIC CAMPUSES
UNIVERSITY EXTENSION
AGRICULTURAL EXTENSION
AGRICULTURAL EXPERIMENT
4-H CENTERS
HOME DEMONSTRATION AGENTS

Above: The 1969 Spring Commencement platform party included U.S. Senator Howard H. Baker, Jr.; George Romney; Dean William Lacey (Architecture); UTK Chancellor Charles Weaver; and UT President Andy Holt. The first degrees in Architecture were awarded.

Left: President Andy Holt blows out the candles on UT's 175th anniversary cake in 1970, while Governor Buford Ellington watches.

Far left: Billy Graham addresses one of 10 Crusade sessions in Neyland Stadium in 1970. The capacity crowd of 75,000 present *(above, top)* when Dr. Graham introduced his invited guest speaker, President Richard Nixon, included Vietnam war protestors *(below, left)* who were arrested for disturbing public worship.

1970 was a year of discontent. In January, police dispersed a crowd of students protesting the selection of Dr. Edward J. Boling as UT President.

Tennessee traditions: *Above, left:* Since designation in 1953, generations of Tennessee blue tick hounds named Smokey have served as the official mascots of the UT Volunteers. Members of the 1971 cheerleading squad (kneeling: Sandy Melrione, John Neal, Jan Campbell; standing: Amy McClain, Pat Green) pose with Smokey before the 1971 season opener. *Above, right:* Pregame enjoyment of the distinctive gait of Tennessee Walking Horses came to an end when artificial turf was found to have the potential to make the horses stumble.

"Those Were The Days": The Reese Hall/Humes Hall group sang their way to victory in All Sing 1975 with a medley which included this popular theme song from <u>All in the Family.</u>

At Right, Seated: UT President Emeritus Andy Holt and President Edward J. Boling. *Standing:* future UT President Joseph E. Johnson (then Executive Vice President and Vice President for Development) and Charles Brakebill, Vice President for Development (then Associate Vice President for Development), 1974.

Fans packed Stokely Athletic Center in 1976 to cheer Coach Ray Mears' "Ernie and Bernie" show. *Far Left:* Bernard King in action at Gainesville, where Tennessee defeated Florida 80-76. *Near left:* Ernie Grunfeld leads the team through the "T". *Above:* Ernie and Bernie share a 1976 cover of *Sports Illustrated*.

1980 view across The Hill to downtown Knoxville shows the landmark tower of Ayres Hall, whose lighting was provided in 1940 by the All Students Club.

On campus in 1980,
Dr. Jack Reese,
UTK Chancellor
1973-1989 and
President Emeritus
Andy Holt (UT
President 1959-
1970).

UTK is one of two major American universities whose football stadiums are accessible by water, and the Vol Navy attends every home game. *Above:* The armada which brought fans to watch the Vols beat Colorado State 42-0 in 1981, rafted out so that fans reach shore and stadium by climbing across the boats.

Left: Leap to the dock, 1980.

Left, top: The Pi Kappa Alpha Fire Truck in the 1983 Homecoming parade. *Left, bottom:* 1979 halftime salute of the Lady Vols by the UT band. *Below:* Fans and goalposts have left the stadium after the 1986 30-0 Vanderbilt victory assured an SEC title and Sugar Bowl trip (Tennessee 35; Miami 7).

Above: Dr. William T. Snyder, UTK Chancellor, is shown
in the early 1980's at the keyboard of the Tennessee
Theatre's "Mighty Wurlitzer" organ, which he began
playing in 1979. The Tennessee Theatre is on the site of
the original Blount College building.

Right: This trombonist in WJ Julian's Pride of the
Southland Marching Band is not marching to a different
drummer — he is moving to join the other trombone
players for practice by instrument.

Above: A world's attendance record
for women's basketball was set at
Thompson/Boling Arena December 9,
1987, when 24,563 spectators
watched the Lady Vols defeat the
Texas Lady Longhorns.

Right: Pat Head Summitt (Lady Vols
Basketball Head Coach since 1974;
Olympic Gold Medal 1984 basketball
team coach) and anxious squad
members watch Tennessee defeat
Auburn 69-65 in the 1991 NCAA
Mid-East Regionals.

Above, Left: ATO Senior Joe Ozment faced strong
competition in the 1988 cake eating competition
sponsored by the Campus Events Committee as
part of Homecoming activities. *Above:* A 2:00 a.m.
shaving cream competition, Hess Hall, 1990.

Above: A second national championship in alternative fuels competition in the 1990 Methanol Car Competition for Dr. Jeffrey Hodgson's Engineering students. *Right:* Dr. Robert Kirk, member of the College of Education faculty since 1967 (first black faculty member on the Knoxville campus) talks with Safety 352 student Andrew Kirk in 1992.

Alex Haley, Adjunct Professor of Communications, talks with (L-R) Billy Stair, UTK Chancellor John Quinn, and UT President Lamar Alexander at Haley's Norris farm, 1989.

Below: In February, 1990, President George Bush was on campus to participate in the announcement of a partnership of the State, UT, Martin Marietta, and the U.S. Department of Energy establishing UTK's "Summer School of the South for Science and Mathematics."

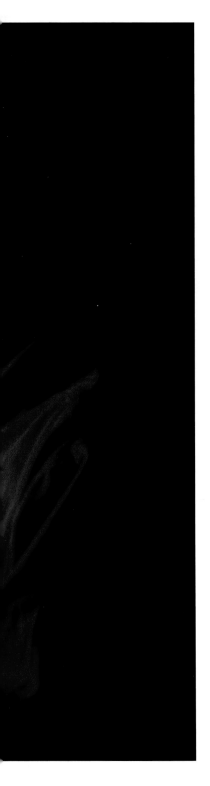

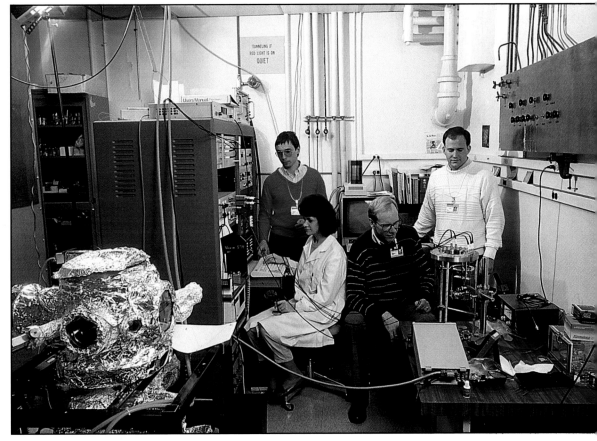

Above: Proximity to the Oak Ridge National Laboratory offers faculty and students unique opportunities to participate in leading edge research, such as this robotics project.

Left: The computer is today a part of the everyday life of students, faculty, and staff.

At right, a 1939
photograph of Dr.
John C. Hodges,
Congreve scholar
and author of the
Harbrace College
Handbook.
Above: Students
in the reference
area of Hodges
Library, 1992.

The ziggurat shape of the John C. Hodges Library, above, takes its place as a campus landmark with the McClung Tower and the classic replica of Europa and the Bull on McClung Plaza.

1991 entry from Sigma Alpha Epsilon in Carnicus, the student skit competition created in 1929 by combining the annual circus and the annual carnival.

Three constants of student life: dormitory bull sessions (here a 1990 Hess Hall, Friday evening example); parking tickets; and a setting in which carrying the torch of learning (symbolized by the Volunteer Statue in Circle Park) is a treasured obligation.

Estabrook Hall served as the first location of the
School of Architecture in the 1960's. *At left*, students line the steps of Estabrook's "Well". The
1981 Art/Architecture Building provides space
for student projects in both art and architecture,
such as *(above)* a 1992 model-building activity.

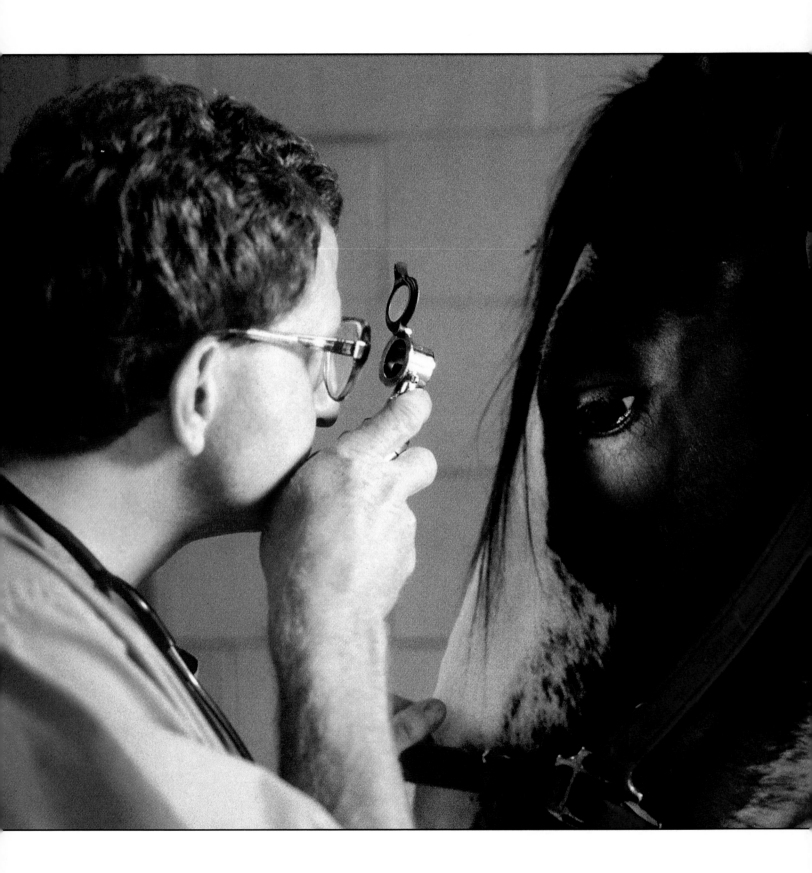

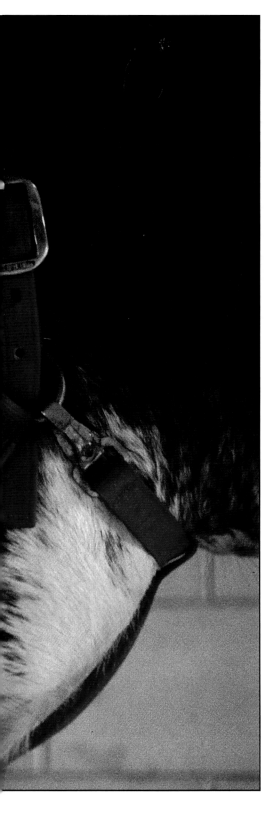

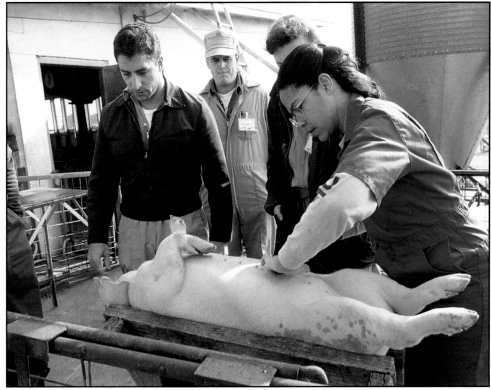

Dr. James Blackford, Associate
Professor of Veterinary
Medicine, conducts part of a
semiannual examination of a
Clydesdale in New Hampshire,
1991. The College has provided
health care consultation for the
Anheuser-Busch Clydesdales
since 1982. *Above:* Veterinary
Medical Resident Dr. Keely
Clare and Vet School student
Michael Renner examine a pig
in preparation for surgery at a
farm in 1992.

Randy Jenkins, member of the 1991 UTK NCAA Championship Track and Field team, clears the bar to win the 1993 NCAA high jump championship after missing the 1992 season while battling Hodgkin's Lymphoma.

The orange wave on its way into Neyland Stadium, 1992.

Tennessee's sixth largest city, on a bright blue day in October, 1993.

Above: The outside of Neyland Stadium, displaying the 1992 version of the annual Homecoming Banner contest, and *(right)* Vol cheerleaders inside the stadium.

Quarterback Heath Shuler, Academic All-SEC and runner-up for the Heisman Trophy, performs some first-quarter acrobatics during the Vols' 45-10 win over Louisville, November 6, 1993. Shuler elected to forgo his senior year to play in the National Football League.

Citrus Bowl, 1994: Loyal Vol fans hoped to cheer the team to victory, but Penn State won 31-13.

From the top of Hodges Library, looking across
the College of Business complex, campus and
city landmarks are visible. At right, Brad Wells,
art major, rollerblading on McClung Plaza.

Don Elder, B.S. in Communications, May, 1993.